My First Animal Library

Jaguars

by Mari Schuh

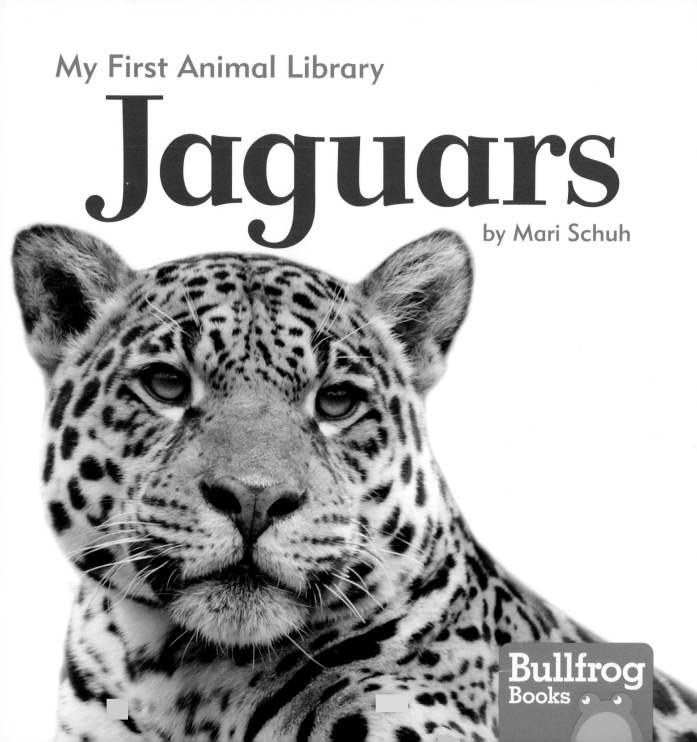

Bullfrog Books

Ideas for Parents and Teachers

Bullfrog Books let children practice reading informational text at the earliest reading levels. Repetition, familiar words, and photo labels support early readers.

Before Reading

- Discuss the cover photo. What does it tell them?

- Look at the picture glossary together. Read and discuss the words.

Read the Book

- "Walk" through the book and look at the photos. Let the child ask questions. Point out the photo labels.

- Read the book to the child, or have him or her read independently.

After Reading

- Prompt the child to think more. Ask: Have you ever seen a jaguar? Can you be as quiet as a jaguar when it hunts? What other things do you think it eats?

Dedicated to St. John Vianney School —MS

Bullfrog Books are published by Jump!
5357 Penn Avenue South
Minneapolis, MN 55419
www.jumplibrary.com

Library of Congress Cataloging-in-Publication Data
Schuh, Mari C., 1975- author.
 Jaguars / by Mari Schuh.
   pages cm.—(My first animal library)
 Summary: "This photo-illustrated book for early readers describes the different ways a jaguar finds food in the rain forest"—Provided by publisher.
 Audience: Ages 5-8.
 Audience: K to grade 3.
 Includes bibliographical references and index.
 ISBN 978-1-62031-111-0 (hardcover)
 ISBN 978-1-62496-178-6 (ebook)
 1. Jaguar—Juvenile literature. I. Title.
 QL737.C23S3465 2014
 599.75'5—dc23
                              2013044260

Editor: Wendy Dieker
Series Designer: Ellen Huber
Book Designer: Lindaanne Donohoe
Photo Researcher: Kurtis Kinneman

Photo Credits: All photos by Shutterstock except: Alamy, 7, 20–21; Ardea/Nick Gordon, 15; Corbis, 16–17; iStockPhoto, 22, 24; SuperStock, 8-9, 12, 14–15, 16, 23bl, 23br, 23 tl

Printed in the United States of America at Corporate Graphics, North Mankato, Minnesota.
6-2014
10 9 8 7 6 5 4 3 2 1

Table of Contents

On the Hunt

A big cat roams the rain forest.

He is a jaguar.

The jaguar hunts for food.

Scratch! Scratch!

He marks his territory.

This is where he lives.

This big cat
hunts alone.

Shh! He is quiet.

He is still.

He is hard to see.

His spots help
him blend in.

The big cat
climbs a tree.

He hunts monkeys.

Splash!

He swims in a river.

He hunts turtles.

turtle · · · · · · ▶

The jaguar waits for his prey.

He sees a deer.

Pounce!

He jumps on it.

prey

Chomp!
He bites with his
strong jaws.

His teeth are sharp.

The jaguar eats
a big meal.

He is full.

He sleeps in a tree.

Parts of a Jaguar

spots
A jaguar's spots help it hide in the shadowy rain forest.

tail
A long tail helps a jaguar keep balance.

jaws
Jaguars have powerful jaws.

Picture Glossary

pounce
To jump on
something
suddenly.

rain forest
A thick area
of trees
where a lot
of rain falls.

prey
Animals that
are hunted
for food.

territory
A large area
of land where
a jaguar lives
and hunts.

Index

To Learn More

Learning more is as easy as 1, 2, 3.

1) Go to www.factsurfer.com

2) Enter "jaguars" into the search box.

3) Click the "Surf" button to see a list of websites.

With factsurfer.com, finding more information is just a click away.